IDEAS Plus

A Collection of Practical Teaching Ideas

Book Fourteen

National Council of Teachers of English
1111 W. Kenyon Road, Urbana, Illinois 61801-1096

Project Coordinator: Felice Kaufmann

Staff Editor: Peter Feely

Cover Design: Joellen Bryant

Interior Book Design: Tom Kovacs for TGK Design

NCTE Stock Number: 22779-3050

Library of Congress Catalog Card Number 84-3479

IDEAS Plus is published in August by the National Council of Teachers of
English as an exclusive benefit of *NCTE Plus* membership. *NCTE Plus* membership also includes four issues of *NOTES Plus* (ISSN 0738-8624), published
in October, December, January, and March. Annual membership dues are
$55.00; $15.00 of this amount is for *NOTES Plus* and *IDEAS Plus*. Inquiries
about *NCTE Plus* membership or communications regarding change of address
and permission to reprint should be addressed to *NOTES Plus*, 1111 W. Kenyon
Road, Urbana, IL 61801-1096. *POSTMASTER:* Send address changes to
NOTES Plus, 1111 W. Kenyon Road, Urbana, IL 61801-1096. Second-class
postage paid at Champaign, Illinois, and at additional mailing offices.

Contents

Foreword

IDEAS Plus and its quarterly companion *NOTES Plus* are the principal benefits of *NCTE Plus* membership. *IDEAS Plus* is sent out at the end of the summer so that teachers will have it in hand as they begin the school year.

The ideas collected in this fourteenth edition of *IDEAS Plus* come from two sources: ideas submitted at an Idea Exchange session at an NCTE Annual Convention or Spring Conference, and contributions by readers of *NOTES Plus* and *IDEAS Plus*.

1 Prewriting and Writing

A rich and varied context for writing helps to connect writing with students' lives. Accordingly, the classroom strategies included in this section cover a wide range of starting points, purposes, and frameworks for writing. Students write in conjunction with reading the newspaper, focusing on the senses, examining comic strips, remembering special trips, and applying for a job, among other activities. Such experiences work towards making writing a lifelong, daily activity while providing the practice and feedback that students need to become confident, effective writers.

Picture Writing

After purchasing about forty black and white photographs from the early 1900s at a shop filled with old paper memorabilia, I developed this two-day creative writing project, in which students write short stories from old photographs.

I bring the photos to class and, as students walk in, ask them to select one. When everyone is seated, I begin class by sharing one of my old photographs with my students. This may be a photo showing me as a child or with family members. The class examines the picture and brainstorms for a few minutes as they imagine what activities transpired immediately before or after the taking of the picture. As a class, we look closely at our pictures, noting facial expressions, background objects, and the relationships between the persons in the picture.

Then I ask the students to write a short story using their selected pictures. Some may choose to write about why the photo was taken; others may choose to write about what happened to the people in the picture.

At the conclusion of this first day, I invite my students to share just their opening paragraphs with the class to create a little suspense.

During the next class period, we display the photos as volunteers take turns reading stories. (The teacher can read stories or excerpts for students who would rather not read their own.) The results are tremendous, and the students seem to enjoy the assignment.

I number the picture and use them for all my classes. And after you've used the assignment once or twice, it can be interesting to read students some examples of different stories that were inspired by the same photos.

Kristina Hoyer, Keith Junior High, Altoona, Pennsylvania

Writing a Thank-You Letter
When You Mean "No, Thank You!"

Right after the winter break is the perfect time for my seventh graders to have a lesson on letter writing—thank-you notes, to be specific. I begin talking about some of the gifts I received for Christmas—some appropriate, some not so appropriate. Students share their memories of recent and past gifts too, and once the ice is broken, everyone feels free to describe even those embarrassing gifts the relatives gave them on their last birthday or holiday. I use this as a "teachable moment" to bring in thank-you letters. I show some examples of thank-you letters and we talk about the proper form for letters and the different parts. Then I bring out a special present.

This special present is a 6" × 8" gift box with a large red bow on top. Someone always wants to know if the present is for them. When I say yes, suddenly everyone is interested. I tell students that the box contains gifts for every one of them. These gifts are from their relatives who ordered them but, because of the overtaxed mail system, were unable to have them delivered by the holidays. So instead, the relatives sent pictures of the gifts. Inside the box are pictures (some accompanied by descriptions) cut from catalogs and magazines and taped to index cards. I carefully choose items that I think will be undesirable as possible to my students, and assign each item the most awful and silly name I can think up.

The students' assignment is to write a thank-you letter in the correct form that tastefully and graciously thanks the sender for the present. I stress that students should find something honestly nice and gracious to say about their gifts, but they can approach the assignment as an imaginative exercise with a touch of humor.

After students complete their letters, we have a voluntary read-aloud session. Nick, for example, was fortunate enough to receive the matching black iron clothes hooks from "Love Muffin and Stud." He wrote, "Since I already have some of these, I now have the perfect anchor for my fishing boat. And guess what? They won't rust either! And since I don't need the mounting screws, I could use them for my new dartboard. How did you know black was my favorite color?"

In my classroom, students who complete a letter receive coupons or other small rewards. Extra credit could also be given. If you have enough time to plan in advance, you can make use of the free mail-order catalogs offered regularly through popular magazines. These provide pictures and descriptions of unusual and humorous items that could be used for gifts—a plastic rock with a secret compartment for a house key or car key; a specially shaped cup for holding dentures while you sleep; a variety of unusual antisnore devices; a whistle that makes duck calls; and so on. Particularly useful are those catalogs that offer a hodgepodge of many different items, such as *Lillian Vernon* and *10,000 Things You Never Knew Existed.*

A possible twist to this activity would be to assemble a variety of catalogs and magazines, scissors, tape, and index cards, and ask students themselves to create the "gifts," which could be exchanged in pairs or selected randomly in a class drawing.

Either way, students enjoy a creative challenge and gain practice in letter writing, and the read-aloud session is enjoyed by all.

Barbara Revor, Conrady Junior High School, Hickory Hills, Indiana

The Poetry-Art Connection

The Poetry-Art Connection is a collaborative project involving writing and art classes. Creativity begins in the English classroom where students write poetry, which is then passed on to the art teacher who instructs students to capture the essence of the poems in drawings. Art students are instructed to imagine themselves in a real-life, on-the-job assignment as illustrators of a book, picking any poem they wish to illustrate. All poems are illustrated.

The artist and the poet never meet until the English classroom puts together a book of art and poetry, whereupon a publication party is held that includes both classes. At the celebration, artwork and poetry are displayed, art-gallery style. Readings are conducted along with "book autographing" by the various "artists"—writers and illustrators.

Shown below are samples of collaborations created by my students. (Collaborations need not be this elaborate.)

Art by Brian Bennett

Awaiting Silent Death

Bloody
at the bottom of the pool
heavy water forces me down
my eyes burn of chlorine, urine
my ears, so full I can hear only
the sounds of my own movements
my fingers
white and wrinkled
helpless hands that cannot pull me
to the surface
my brain
near implosion
feels the water's icy teethmarks
leave behind frozen tatoos.

I can see the sun shining
through my liquid window
unable to feel its warmth,
because I'm trapped
behind the glass.

Ann Berman

The Lemonade Summers

It's those dog days of summer
I so fondly remember
sipping soury-sweet lemonade
at a sale in my yard.
The white birch trees
as full as a petticoat
shade us from the firey sun.
Fingers as sticky
as kindergarden glue
wrap around ice cold glasses
where beads of water
like our beads of sweat
roll down the last
lemony drop of the drinks
we made.

Eden Downs

Art by Megan Sember

Since students compose in many ways, drawing becomes a form of construct that represents the artist's version of reality. The artist becomes an interpreter of the poem; and the writing, which is no longer for the teacher's consumption, now has a life of its own, one that is capable of generating multiple levels of meaning that can be comprehended by different audiences.

Having their poems illustrated raises the confidence level of writers who see the worthiness of their work reflected in the grandiosity of a drawing. And writers are both pleased and surprised by the multiple levels of meaning their poetic lines are capable of generating.

In a high school, a student of art is also a student of English; consequently, both transact with the text, producing *enactments* of text through their elevation from mere students to that of poets and artists. When students put together the book of poetry and art, they assume the role of publishers, making critical judgements about the placement of one work in relation to another.

Assessment can take place in a variety of ways, depending upon the goals of the assignment. Students can be evaluated on the roles they assume in compiling the publication of the class book—planning the layout, writing a dedication or a "literary review," as well as a host of other organizational roles that integrate their creative talents with the goals of the lesson.

Marilyn Bates, Mount Lebanon Schools, Pittsburgh, Pennsylvania

A more detailed treatment of this assignment appeared in the February 1995 issue of English Journal.

Setting the Scene for a Unique Writing Experience

Many English teachers have encouraged their students to make their writing vivid and realistic by "painting with words." For those students who must actually experience something concrete before they under-stand this concept, the following exercise is an enjoyable activity which will help them understand and practice "using their senses."

This activity works best if you enlist two student helpers ahead of time. You will need large candles and candleholders; incense; peppermint (or another strong-tasting) candy; an overhead projector and screen; a clear glass bowl; liquid food coloring; any kind of clear vegetable oil; a straw; and music. (Any instrumental music will work, but the best is instrumental music that carries varied and intense moods. I have used Tchaikovsky's *Nutcracker Suite* with success.)

If feasible, push all the desks out into the hall or into one corner of the room. Pull the blinds or cover the windows, making the room as dark as possible. Fill the bowl with water and put it on the projector where the transparency ordinarily goes. When you turn on the projector, you should see the round surface of the water on the screen. Place the lighted candles on the floor around the room and light the incense.

The class waits in the hall until everyone is assembled. (They have been told only to bring paper and pencil.) Finally, the door is opened; each student is given a piece of candy; the music soars; the incense permeates the room; the candles make shadows on the walls. Into this strange environment tiptoe the awestruck students who follow quiet directions to sit on the floor and face the screen. It is now time for your student helpers to practice their artistry. (Give them any necessary instructions in advance so as not to detract from the mood.) They add drops of color/oil and stir/blow the water to match the mood of the music until it ends or until the water has turned black.

Finally, the teacher turns on the lights and the students write a description of their experience which they then share with the class.

Each student will respond to this experience in his/her unique way. Some may think of nature or of images from dreams or from poetry. Others may focus on abstract moods or on people or events brought to mind by the music. Some students may have felt the music and candlelight had a soothing, lulling effect on them, while others may have felt awakened and invigorated by the new experiences. Students can be reassured that each person's interpretation is valid.

This exercise is valuable for several reasons. First, it helps students put their sense impressions into writing. Second, it motivates them to use specific, exact words to describe their unique perspective. Third, it helps them value their own and their classmates' interpretations of a shared experience. And last, it's a fun and stimulating change of pace.

Judith Cunningham, Eastern Kentucky University, Richmond, Kentucky

"Can We Have One More Day to Revise? Please?"

"Can we have one more day to revise? Please?"

"Are you sure we get a grade for this?"

"We get to draw in language arts?"

When was the last time your middle school students spent three days on writing revisions and then begged for just one more day to revise? This writing activity is guaranteed to turn any thirteen-year-old into a revision maniac.

The basis for this writing assignment is "Dragon, Dragon," John Gardner's zany fairy tale about a kingdom plagued by a prank-playing dragon whose favorite pastime is sneaking into people's homes and tearing the last chapter out of all their novels. After reading "Dragon, Dragon" with my middle school students, we discuss, in detail, what Gardner's dragon looks like. A lively discussion ensues with much disagreement about the actual physical description of the dragon. Students then search the text of the story for clues and discover that Gardner does not offer any. He carefully documents all the actions of the dragon, but ignores any actual physical description of it. How can a reader glean an image from a text without careful guidance from the writer? Students soon realize that they developed a picture of this main character based on his actions in the story coupled with the preconceived picture of what

dragons look like from their own imaginations. Thus we begin to explore what pictures students bring to the story.

Journal Writing

In their writing journals students describe the dragon that lives in their imaginations. They describe its personality and appearance in as much detail as possible. Students share their journal entries with the class, contrasting and comparing their dragons. Journals are retired, and students begin their preliminary drawing of their dragons. Reluctant artists are encouraged and reassured by peers and teacher.

Sketch and Describe Dragon

After the first sketches are complete, students write a detailed description telling their reader how to draw their dragon. Students are directed to write with such precision that another student will be able to reproduce the original dragon by reading the written description only. Everyone insists that they can easily do this, so they eagerly share their first drafts.

"You didn't say which way your dragon is facing on the page. What is the shape of his head? You said he had wings. Where are they connected to his body? What shape are they?" Students quickly discover which areas of their descriptions need more detail.

Peer Editing

The next day students work in pairs to polish their drafts. Peer editors are directed to read each text several times and list all questions as they arise. I encourage students to have someone at home draw their dragon from their descriptions as a final editing procedure that night.

Drawing from Description

The next day is the true test of the effectiveness of the description. All classes turn in the pictures with their written descriptions before school starts. I switch all four classes' papers. Each student must read a description and reproduce the dragon that is described on the page. The next day I post all original drawings and the drawings produced by the reader of the piece side by side with the written description. The students can't wait to see the results of their hard work.

Class Evaluation and Discussion

We discuss the "good, the bad, and the ugly." Why are some reproductions so close to the originals? Occasionally, the student interpreting the written description is a great artist, but primarily, clear and well-organized written descriptions result in good pictures. The descriptions are precise and free of extraneous facts. The directions follow a logical order and are devoid of contradictory information.

Closure

Students return to their drafts for one last revision using the comments and drawing of their peer editor as a guide. I evaluate the final papers based on each student's improvement of successive drafts.

Creating a visual image from someone's draft is an excellent illustration of what happens when a reader tries to derive meaning from a piece of writing. The students can easily "see" the mistakes of their peers and also have proof of their own needs for revision. This activity validates the need for the revision process in writing. Students learn to value their use of language and realize that effective communication requires dedication, patience, and careful attention to details and audience.

Beth Lockwood, Nipher Middle School, Kirkwood, Missouri

Cooperative Story Assignment

This assignment is a progressive group story for writing groups of four or five students each. It can be used with students at many levels, and is most effective after the class has studied story elements and has had ample practice identifying these elements in literature activities. It takes two or three class periods to complete.

To begin, have the class brainstorm ideas for various elements and details that could be used in creating a story—specific settings ("the state fair," "an old house by the river," "a sunny beach in Florida"), character details such as number, age, sex ("three elderly sisters living together," "a teenage boy and girl on vacation with their families," "a little boy who doesn't talk"), and basic plot ideas and approaches ("the main character thinks someone is after him/her," "the character(s) get caught in a big storm," "the main character finds a briefcase full of money").

Accept all suggestions and write them on the board or on an overhead transparency. Cluster related ideas and use discussion to eliminate items that are less workable. When enough clusters are developed so that the writing groups have some selection, ask each group to choose a cluster for more individual-group expansion and refinement.

Explain that each group will need to choose a Recorder, a Reporter, a Gofer, and one or two Encouragers. The Recorder will record all the ideas in the group's cluster, plus any other ideas the group wants to add; the Reporter will read the finished story aloud to the class; the Gofer will pass materials around, ask questions of the teacher if necessary, and run any errands that are needed; and the Encouragers will give general encouragement to the group members, suggest when the group should move on to the next step, and help to keep the group running smoothly.

Each group will first need to spend a few minutes discussing the elements in their cluster. They may want to agree on certain additional details such as character names, place names, and so on before the first student begins writing. Then the group Recorder begins by writing the first section of the story, using the elements in the group's cluster. (For the writing portion of the activity to be completed in one class period, each student will need to write his or her section in five to seven minutes.) Then the Recorder reads his or her section to the group, and the story is passed around clockwise for all members of the group to write and read in turn until everyone agrees it is complete.

At that point, the Reporter of each group is to read the story aloud, paragraph by paragraph, for group discussion and revision. Once all revisions are completed, each member of the group takes a part of the story to edit. The edited story is passed around the group so that at least two group members read and edit all parts. The Recorder of each group makes a final copy of the corrected composition for sharing and filing in the group's folder.

During the next class period, each group's Reporter reads the group's final story to the class for response and evaluation.

This exercise contains all the essentials of the writing process and provides vital experience in group process as well. I have found that the students readily become involved and enjoy the outcome because they have the security of not being alone in the effort.

Susie Moody, Marshfield Junior High School, Marshfield, Michigan

Stripping Writing to the Main Points

While attending a high school teachers' workshop on writing proficiency at the University of Michigan, Ann Arbor, I participated in a discussion about writing skills that are important for college students. Naturally, some of the key skills identified were the ability to read, analyze and respond to articles, opinions, and theories. In an effort to help high school students develop proficiency in these skills, I developed the following assignment and used it with my sophomore English classes. This assignment helps students to focus on identification and development of main ideas, and strengthens summary and comparison writing skills.

The teacher first chooses an article or editorial that advances a point of view. I try to select something that is well organized into main points and that presents a subject the students have heard about. Another criterion is finding an article that is not too lengthy. The editorial page of a daily newspaper is a good source for finding appropriate materials.

Students are asked to skim copies of the articles and list the main ideas and overall view of the author. Many students have difficulty with this first basic step. To assist students, I copy the article onto an overhead, and we identify main points and ideas as a class. Students compare this list to their original list.

Students are asked to write a two-paragraph draft based on this article, in which they adhere to the following format. In the first paragraph, students introduce the article, author, date, and subject of discussion. They present each main point in the same order the author did, with a brief explanation of the author's ideas on this point, and end with the author's overall view on the subject. In the second paragraph, students present their opinion or reaction to each main point in turn, and end with their overall view of the subject.

Students then participate in a peer editing session, in which they also note whether the student authors followed the format for presenting points and responses. Students revise their writing, prepare a final copy, and turn it in along with the draft and the two lists of main points they started with.

Because this assignment strips the writing process down to identifying the main points and responding, it's easier for students to focus on these two tasks. And the specific structure and brevity of the writings make it easy to evaluate and discuss them, whether in the context of peer editing, whole-class discussion, or review by the teacher.

Katherine McClain, Garden City Junior High School Garden City, Michigan

Comic Strips Prompt Writing

This assignment serves as an effective and entertaining introduction to the narrative essay. Using comic strips, students are invited to draw inferences and inventively impose layers of complexity on the simple form. The cartoon's inherent narrative structure is a natural taking-off point for imagining richer narratives.

I obtained this strategy while swapping ideas at a conference last year, though I can't remember whose idea it was originally. I've used it for two semesters and students always enjoy it.

After the class has read and discussed several narrative essays, we all look at a four-frame comic strip together. We describe the characters in the strip and their relationship to each other, consider the setting, speculate as to the thoughts and emotions of the characters if they are not spelled out, and narrate the incident presented in the strip.

Then I provide each student with his or her own self-contained, four-frame comic strip that includes at least two characters and a dialogue. I give students the following worksheet to complete in class:

Where and when is the cartoon set?

Describe each of the characters.

What is the relationship of the characters to each other?

What mood or emotion does each character display?

What is each character thinking?

What is each character saying?

What happens in this cartoon?

After students have fully answered these questions, they pick up this essay assignment:

Your task is to take the cartoon episode you discussed in Part I and turn it into a narrative essay. In your first paragraph, present the setting and introduce the situation.

You will notice that your cartoon contains some dialogue. Please remember the conventions of writing dialogue: the use of paragraphs and quotation marks. Your second and third paragraphs, at least, will present the conversation of your characters along with their thoughts and their actions.

Your final paragraph will show the outcome of the situation you have described.

Students draft their essays outside of class, and then spend class time in peer editing, revision, and sharing the results.

Dorothy Beck, Black Hawk College, Moline, Illinois

Memories of Trips, Vacations, and Special Moments

In this project, students focus on memories of trips, vacations, and other special moments through writing and oral presentations. To make certain that all my students can become actively and positively involved, I emphasize that "memories" is a broad category that can include many different kinds of special moments with friends and relatives. Another option for students, instead of focusing on their own memories, is to sit down with a friend or neighbor to capture that person's memories of a trip or special moment.

When I used this project with my sixth and seventh graders, I first requested that students bring in an item of memorabilia from a trip, vacation, or special moment. Students and I brainstormed what might be considered memorabilia. Among the items we came up with were souvenirs, toys, trip maps, banners, t-shirts, mugs, emblemed caps, leaves/dried flowers, currency, ticket stubs, menus, and so on.

On the day we brought in our items, the students' desks as well as my own table were filled with photos, photo albums, fast food souvenirs, invitations, place cards, figurines, towels, foreign language newspapers, and assorted other items. The students were excited and eager to talk about their memorabilia. We spent that class period and the next in informal oral presentations, giving each of the students a chance to explain the origin and significance of their item(s). The objects were reverentially passed around and examined by class members. As part of the oral presentation, students could also ask questions about the items such as where they came from.

By the time the second class period ended, the student presenters were ready to sit down and write about their objects. With their items in hand, students spent a full class period recording their memory and their feelings about it. In contrast to our usual writing sessions, where there were always a few students who didn't know what to write, everyone sat and wrote.

Given the rich oral discussion, peer response, and additional time for student reflection, I was not surprised by the quality and quantity of the writing that resulted. Here are two examples from students' work:

Marisol's Snowy Day

This photo was taken during our first winter in the Bronx. My sisters and I were born in San Juan, Puerto Rico. We had never experienced snow. When I was five and my sisters three and four, we moved to the Bronx. I remember sitting by the window and watching my very first snow flakes fall. It looked like a film on television picture, but somewhere inside I knew this was real.

Suddenly Mommy came in with our new winter coats and mittens. . . . Mommy said "Out you go . . . go roll in the snow, make snow angels." I couldn't believe that we were going to enter into the picture. My sisters and I were going to become part of that beautiful scene. It seemed magical.

Barry

We always go to my Grandma who lives in Shirley, Long Island during the summer and some weekends in June. The first time I ever went there, my Dad woke me up early on Saturday and told me he was going to take me somewhere that Grandpa used to take him when he was a child. I never knew Grandpa. He died before I was born so I knew Dad was doing this to remember his own Dad. My Dad really missed Grandpa, even though he died over 15 years ago.

Anyway, Dad and I got into the car and left Mommy, my Grandpa, and sisters at home asleep. We went to a big diner called The Golden Rule that you had to climb two flights of stairs to get into. The diner was big inside with juke boxes at each table and place mats with games. It looked nice, but I had been to places like it in Brooklyn.

When I asked Dad what was the special he smiled. Then he ordered for us. The waitress came over with a big plate of large sandwiches. The sandwich let off heat so I could almost not see what was inside it. My dad said his dad always had him close his eyes, open his mouth wide, and bite down. My Dad and I both did that. The sandwich was the best fried egg on roll sandwich I ever had. It was humongous! We had egg creams with it. For dessert we had freshly baked plain donuts from the oven.

Dad said that only the Golden Rule made sandwiches and donuts like that. They had been doing it since he was my age. We brought back some donuts for Grandma, Mommy, and my sisters, but these donuts were cooled off by the time we got back. Whenever we go to Shirley, Long Island, Dad and I go to the Golden Rule by ourselves. I brought in the menu from the restaurant.

As a follow-up to students' writing, I told students that if they would like, they could take their writings home and ask a family member to write, share, or dictate their perspective on the memory.

Soon after, we published a class memory book in which we included not only the original student pieces but some of their relatives' memories as well. To celebrate our publication, we held a festival in the gym where we exhibited the original memorabilia, along with the writings.

A few of our students' family members offered to bring in family movies, slides, albums, and cassettes that related to the same memories. At first I hesitated, but when I asked the class as a whole what they thought, I found that most of them were eager to see and hear more of the background for the class writings. Ultimately, not only was the project a success in terms of the writings and oral presentations, but family and community bonds were cemented through this collaborative effort.

Rose Reissman, Community School District #1, Brooklyn, New York

A Stuffed Man Sparks Writing, or "Hey, Who *Is* That Kid?!"

I had a stuffed man sitting outside my house as a Halloween decoration, and when it was over I thought I'd bring him to school to see how long it would take my students to realize he was not real. I sat him in a desk with his head down. He had on a gray hooded sweatshirt. Some kids caught on right away. Others . . . well it was quite a laugh when after three days a student said to me, "Hey, who is that kid?"

He was given the name "Maynard," and he spent the rest of the semester with us. The expression, "Don't be a Maynard!" became commonplace. About a week into Maynard's stay I had the students complete the following assignment, with very good results.

You've applied for a job at Joe's Shop and Eat a Lot. The hours are 3:00–6:00 Monday–Friday. The pay is $15.00 per hour. You really want this job because the hours are perfect for your busy schedule, and the pay is excellent.

As Joe looked through the applications he came up with two very qualified individuals, you and Maynard. He just couldn't decide who to hire, so he asked you to write a comparison/contrast letter to him, explaining why he should hire you for the position.

We spent time on the basics of comparison/contrast prior to this lesson, and had previously worked quite a bit on successful use of transitional words and phrases. Through this lesson students were able not only to work on an important skill but also to say some good things about themselves in writing.

Tricia LeRoy, Columbia Heights Alternative Program, Columbia Heights, Minnesota

Walking in Someone Else's Shoes

Because I teach several different levels, I needed to invent a creative writing activity that worked for different age groups and abilities. This

Walking in Someone Else's Shoes
Handout Page

1. Give the owner a first, middle, and last name:

2. Age:

3. Marital status:

4. What does the owner look like? (Give details)

5. What does the owner do for a living? (e.g., does the owner work a nine-to-five job; is he or she a student, an athlete, a movie star, a musician, a manicurist, a hematologist?)

6. Where does the owner live and with whom?

7. List three personality traits of the owner:

8. What does the owner do in his or her spare time?

9. What is the owner's favorite food?

10. What is the owner's favorite book?

11. What is the owner's favorite movie?

12. Name one bad habit the owner has:

13. How do other people feel about the owner?

is it! I bring in five different types of shoes including a cowboy boot, a high-heeled pump, a basketball sneaker, a beach sandal, and an oxford-type shoe. I borrow the shoes from family, friends, and neighbors so as to get specimens from all "walks of life."

I divide the class into five cooperative learning groups and hand each group a shoe. After examining their shoe for about five minutes, the students are to envision the owner and complete the handout sheet (see Page 23).

When finished analyzing the owner, the students share their answers in class. There are always a lot of laughs as students reveal details about the invented owners, such as Harry Evandorf whose favorite movie is *Forrest Gump* and who can be found hidden behind *Money* magazine smoking a Cuban cigar. After all the groups have introduced their owners, I disclose information about the *actual* owner of each shoe. The students love to hear how close or how far-off they were to describing the real owner.

In order to put this activity to good use, the students then take their shoe questionnaire and write either a short story or a poem about the owner. The stories and poems incorporate the personality traits and lifestyle of the invented owner. I have found "Walking in Someone Else's Shoes" to be an excellent precursor to any creative writing activity.

Kimberly A. Dana, Upper Marion High School, King of Prussia, Pennsylvania

2 Literature

Finding ways to get students to read is great, but clearly the point is not simply to rack up page counts. We want students to read not as passive vessels but with alert and interested minds, able to evaluate, corroborate, even dispute what they read. The strategies included in this section help students move toward more active reading by involving them in questioning, discussing, and evaluating the ideas and language in what they read. Students can savor the satisfaction of reading even as they hone their abilities to read carefully and critically.

Finding Poetry in the Music of the Day

Here's an assignment that students work hard at and enjoy. I challenge the students to find poetry and excellence in the music of the day, to prove to me that their generation is capable of producing thoughtful, profound literature, words that are significant in thought. I ask them to:

1. Find a musical group or star that you enjoy. Listen carefully to the words of each song. Find a song that has a philosophy, a point of view, a definite message to it, but no profane language.
2. Get one copy of the words of the song for everyone in the class.
3. Analyze the song for its deeper meaning, its philosophy. Then find one piece of literature (or a philosophy of an era) that we have studied that reflects a similar or opposing philosophy.
4. Write a short essay comparing the two pieces, to be presented to the class orally.

This assignment takes about seven days. We take two or three days to find and explore a song. We do this right in class. I bring in old records for those who cannot find their own (this has rarely been necessary in my class); and we play the music as we search. I give students two or three days to write their papers in class as I confer with each. We take the last three or four days of school to present these papers to the class and play the music in the background.

I am always amazed at the diversity of music that is selected, as well as at the messages that music sends. I have had selections such as Jethro Tull's "The Story of the Hare Who Lost His Spectacles," UB40's "Desert Sand," The Beatles' "She's Leaving Home," and Guns and Roses' "The Little Children."

One student compared Pink Floyd's "On Turning Away" to Alfred Lord Tennyson's "Lady of Shalott."

> "On Turning Away" is a song about how society today turns away from those who are troubled. . . . We are so driven by the American Dream that we don't see how many people need our help. . . . This song questions society itself. Is life only a dream? The choice must come from the inside. . . . The Lady of Shalott was a person who could do . . . nothing but watch. Even if she saw, she could only be a spectator. . . . She was driven by her dream and found herself alone in pursuing the ideal life. . . . And as she floated down the river, society saw her, but did not see. They turned away.

Another compared the song "She" by Green Day to the women of the Victorian Age. She wrote that like the woman in the song, the Victorian ladies must have "screamed in silence" because they were "locked in a world that's been planned out . . . feeling like a social fool without a use. . . ."

The students enjoy the chance to show me that what they listen to has meaning. It's interesting for them to see how the lyrics and ideas of popular music compare to what they have studied all year—they find it amazing that many of these songs contain the same ideas used by the writers of the past.

Karen Kurzman, North County Union High School, Newport, Vermont

Advice from Polonius and Parents

In *Hamlet*, Act I, Sc. iii, Polonius gives advice to Laertes, who is about to return to France.

Before my seniors have read this scene, I ask them to give the following "writing prompt" to their parents. (Students who don't live with their parents can ask an older friend or relative to complete this step.)

Imagine that I am going off to college tomorrow morning. Write a letter to me, giving me any advice you want me to have.

Parents have been very responsive to this "assignment." On the day the advice is due, students read or summarize what their parents or relatives have written. Discussion follows the readings. We look for common ideas and concerns and group them on the board or overhead. Some categories are

Relating to roommate/strangers

Enjoyment of the college experience

Importance of finding a job or profession they love

Assurance of belief in the child

Emphasis on safety and caution

Importance of letters and phone calls

Assurance that child will be missed

Next, we consider the passage from *Hamlet*. I ask the class which part of Polonius's advice they believe is the best. Invariably, they choose the final lines:

> "... to thine own self be true,
> And it must follow, as the night the day,
> Thou canst not then be false to any man."

I ask them if they believe the lines logically conclude the advice he stated in the previous part of the passage. Students realize that the final lines are somewhat contradictory to the rest of the speech in which Polonius tells Laertes how to act, blend with the crowd and, in effect, follow the safe, conventional path.

Unlike Polonius's advice, the parents' advice is usually characterized by warmth, love, trust and sincerity. In most cases, the parents' respect for the child's individuality is reflected in the advice they offer. In contrast to Polonius, most parents express belief in their child's own judgment. Tone and content differences are discovered.

The activity leads to lively dialogue in class. Students enjoy their parents' involvement, and have definite ideas on what advice should be given, what advice teenagers in general need, and what kind of advice is most likely to be effective. In addition, the characterization of Polonius is established, and Shakespeare comes closer to kids' lives.

Linda B. Owen, Orchard Park High School, Orchard Park, New York

Hats Off to Reading—and to Hats!

Questions: How do I get my students to really feel what they are reading? How can I get the students closer to the characters in the story?

Answer: Fill your room with hats!

Countless actors have stated that it was the hat that finished off the character and made them truly feel the part. With a little ingenuity, you can give your students the same edge.

You can start by looking for hats in thrift shops, flea markets, estate sales, garage sales, and so on. It is here where you will tend to find the hats of American literature. Look for the hats of *Daisy Miller,* Arthur Miller's characters in *Death of a Salesman,* or ask yourself: what kind of hat would you wear if you were at Walden pond? The list goes on and on.

It will be harder to find hats (but don't give up) to accompany British literature, but many of these can be made if you put your mind to it, or if you enlist the skills of a talented friend or student. Students interested in history may very well be willing to do some period research and plan some authentic hats for classroom wear. Check local fabric stores for patterns, remnants, and advice on creating, decorating, and caring for hats. One way to protect the hats is to use a fabric protector on them, but beware—not all fabrics can be protected.

If you are lucky enough to have a school that has a theater department, they may be able to loan hats out to you. If your school is close to a college or university you might check to see if you can borrow hats from their theater department, or if they could donate remnants of fabric, ribbon, lace, etc. that could be used in making or refurbishing hats. The costume department might also be able to offer advice and recommend sources for pictures of hats from different periods.

As you start collecting these hats, you'll need to find a way to hang and display them when they're not in use during class time. Look for a hat rack or two at local flea markets, auctions, or secondhand stores. Or check with the woodshop instructor at your school for ideas—could a handy student be enlisted to make a simple hat rack? Or could the instructor suggest a simple design and the materials needed? You will also need several large boxes for stacking hats at the end of the day and, preferably, access to a lockable storage cabinet or closet to store the hats during off hours.

It is important that you make these hats visible and accessible to your students, but you'll also need to lay down ground rules to protect both hats and students. The hats are meant to be enjoyed, but let students know that they shouldn't be handled carelessly (particularly if they are borrowed). They aren't toys—their purpose is to help create the sense of certain characters and time periods, and to help students "put on" and "take off" the roles of literary characters in order to gain a deeper understanding of them.

And if you and your students truly develop a hat fetish, you'll find a variety of other ways that hats can be used to enhance reading and literature—improvisational dialogues between characters from a story or novel, with hats used to distinguish among characters; wall or table displays of student-created hats that try to capture the essence of certain characters; "period displays" based on historical stories or novels, including hats, pictures, drawings, and other items that illustrate life and customs at that time; and so on. The possibilities are endless, so hats off to reading—and to hats!

Kip Gansneder, West Virginia University, Morgantown

Sneaking Students into Symbolism and Theme

As a teacher of literature, I always have a couple of important goals in mind. I want my students to do real writing in connection with what they read, rather than simply writing answers to questions. I also want them to make their own meaning out of what they read and to discover for themselves the beauty of great literature. But achieving these goals consistently is easier said than done, especially when I am wanting my students to pick up abstract ideas like symbolism and theme. One way to allow students to discover symbolism and theme on their own as well as create a real piece of writing is to "sneak" them into it using what I have called the "character-item poem."

Despite the boring name, my students had fun with this assignment while we were studying Lorainne Hansberry's play, *A Raisin in the Sun*. After we read the first scene in class, I asked my students to respond to this important scene by writing a poem. I gave them a few possibilities, but the overwhelming majority chose the "character-item" poem. For this poem, they were to choose one character from the play and then think of some item that could be associated with the character based on what is known about him or her from the first scene. I told them that it did not necessarily have to be an object explicitly referred to in the play. Then I asked them to write about that item using the following formula:

LINE 1—*State the item's name*
LINE 2—*Give a literal description of it*
LINE 3—*Give a figurative description of it*
LINE 4—*Give one adjective for it*
LINE 5—*Give another adjective for it*
LINE 6—*State what the thing does for the person*
LINE 7—*Give a final description (adj. then noun)*

After we discussed the formula a bit, the students were ready to write. And write they did! I was surprised and impressed by their word choice, imagery, and ability to hit upon abstract ideas never mentioned in class. They were surprised at how well their pieces turned out and how much they enjoyed it. D. J. wrote:

"Mama's Flower"

Mama's flower,
Live plant that needs water and sun to survive,
Holder of her hopes and dreams,

Living,
Growing,
Allows Mama to grow her dreams,
Beautiful hope.

This poem and others like it (about one fourth of the class chose to write their poem about this same plant) led to a wonderful discussion of Mama's plant as a central symbol in the play and helped students feel confident about identifying other symbols as well. I was surprised to notice that several students chose an intangible item for their "character-item" poem. Mandy wrote:

"Dreams"

Dreams,
Goals, ambitions,
Unreached destinations crying out for new inhabitants,
Grandiose,
Frivolous,
Reasons for living,
Wistful "if's."

This poem as well as others similar to it guided our discussion of theme. Thanks to this writing assignment, my students dove into the beauty of Hansberry's play and came back with something beautiful that they had created themselves. The success of my "character-item" poem was proven to me, ironically, the day *before* the poems were turned in. One student, obviously very proud of her work, rushed over to me before class to show me a rough draft of her poem. Speaking quickly and excitedly, she said, "I got in trouble for working on this during history, but I just couldn't put it down!"

Mary Ann Steutermann, Assumption High School, Louisville, Kentucky

Literary Dialogues via Computer

This activity employs several different pedagogical techniques. I have used it in a sophomore world literature class with novels such as *Things Fall Apart* by Chinua Achebe, *Nectar in a Sieve* by Kamala Markandaya, and *A Tale of Two Cities* by Charles Dickens.

Students read the novel, and we spend a good deal of time discussing the characters. Since our courses are team taught (English, history, and religion), students have also spent time looking at current world events. The assignment is to choose a character from the novel (e.g., Rukmani from *Nectar in a Sieve*) and create a conversation between that character and a real person in current news, such as a politician, an activist, a business leader, a film director, etc.

Students pair up and meet during class in the computer lab. Each pair shares one computer, and each student takes the part of one character. For more authentic dialogues, students will need to have on hand these references for information about their character and person: a copy of the story or novel and a copy of one or more newspaper or magazine articles about the real person (with direct quotations from that person if possible).

Together, the two students create a dialogue using each character's appropriate voice. The object is to speak and think as these characters might in this fictitious setting; the dialogue should be meaningful—that is, more than just a trivial exchange of greetings. Dialogues should include references to characters' own experience (novel or reality), preferably weaving these references naturally into the conversation rather than simply tacking them on.

In the process of writing dialogues, students must look more closely at their characters and at what gives each one a unique voice, thus gaining insights into how characters are developed. Students also benefit from their discussion of current events, their examination of their sources (novel or story, newspaper articles) for support, and their collaborative experience at computer-assisted writing.

Steven Billeau, Seattle Preparatory School, Seattle, Washington

Poetry Performances

Here's an assignment that engages students in reflection, critical analysis, and using their creativity. It works well as part of a poetry unit or after students have read works by a diverse group of poets.

First ask students to select a favorite poem or series of poems and to write a short introduction explaining why they chose this poem or series and what they like best about it.

Next, as homework, ask students to try reading their poems aloud. Challenge them to think about and try out different voices and tones of voice. They should practice several times, possibly in front of the mirror or a family member or friend, until they feel comfortable reading the poem aloud.

At this point, tell students they have the option of turning their poetry reading into a recording on audiocassette or into a performance on video. The video performance could involve a simple reading to music or a more complicated staged version of the poem. Ask students to consider which medium would work best for the type of poem they chose, as well as what props or special preparations would be necessary for each format. (This step can be limited to recording on audiocassette or to classroom performance if necessary.)

For students choosing to make an audiocassette recording, ask them to think about whether they would like to add sound effects or play a popular song or other appropriate background music while they read. They'll probably need to make a few practice recordings before making the final tape, in order to check sound level, determine the desired pace, work out the timing of any sound effects, and so on. Once students choose this format, they begin work planning the actual recording with a partner and several spare cassettes.

Students choosing to shoot a video will need to storyboard various scenes and select a shooting site. If the video will require additional actors, student auditions may be held, and the director/producer and his or her assistant will need to cast the parts and provide direction. Should students want to use sound effects or a sound track, they can enlist others to help coordinate prerecording a tape of sound effects or music or playing live music during the videotaping.

Whatever format your students choose, planning and performing poetry readings (and viewings) is an exciting and rewarding project—it's a hands-on way for students to learn to appreciate poetry.

Rose Reissman, Community School District #1, Brooklyn, New York

"Shakespeare" Music

In order to counteract the inevitable "Why Do We Have to Study This Old, Dead Guy" syndrome in my freshmen English classes, I usually start my Shakespeare unit off with music.

To begin the unit, we spend one class period discussing what everyone knows, and what they want to know, about Shakespeare. Then I go into my little spiel about Shakespeare's influence in our culture—his inventive language, his memorable characters, and his pervasive influence on theater, opera, and ballet. Additionally, I share with my students a description of Kansas City's Heart of America Shakespeare Festival and invite them to attend (for free) in the summer.

Finally, I mention that Shakespeare has even influenced popular music in our day—nearly four hundred years after his death. I then play the music and challenge the students to match the references in the music with the list of plays on the board. After this activity is completed, I ask the students to listen for references to Romeo and/or Juliet in the rest of the musical selections.

We spend the remainder of the period listening to music from the list below. In subsequent days while the students delve more deeply into the historical context and get a taste of Elizabethan language and vocabulary, I play more of the music and take requests for favorite pieces to be replayed.

For many years this musical introduction to Shakespeare has served to create in my students positive expectations about the unit. The students often leave the classroom humming or singing snatches of music from the pieces they've heard.

The following list is not an extensive one; however, as Mercutio says after being fatally wounded by Tybalt: "Tis enough, twill serve."

From the musical *Kiss Me, Kate:* "Brush Up Your Shakespeare"

Diamond Rio, *Close to the Edge:* "This Romeo Ain't Got His Julie Yet"

Bon Jovi: "Always"

Troop, *I'm Not Soupped:* "Still in Love"

Dolly Parton and Friends: "Romeo"

Madonna: "Cherish"

Dire Straits: "Romeo and Juliet"

Wilson Phillips: "Next to You—Someday I'll Be"

Patty Loveless: "I'm That Kind of Girl"

Blue Oyster Cult: "(Don't Fear) The Reaper"

Carol Mahieu, Northeast Magnet High School, Kansas City, Missouri

Character Assessment Assignment

In this assignment, students use a character assessment sheet to rank the importance of various values for literary characters, supporting their decisions with evidence from the novel. I have used this assignment with a wide range of novels, usually as a culminating activity. I have also used it twice with the same novel, once after students had read half of the book and then again at the end of the novel. Used in this way, the assignment served as a vehicle to focus attention on the character development in the book. It's important that students work with a character who has a significant role in the book, so I usually provide a list of several characters from which students can choose.

Before students begin filling out the sheet, I ask them to look over my preliminary list of values. I invite them to ask about any terms they are unfamiliar with, and to suggest any additional values they might want to add to the list. These can be added in the blanks provided.

Character Assessment Sheet

Values are principles or ideals which individuals or groups consider important in guiding their lives. Listed here are values which a person might consider important. Select *five* that you believe _____ (character's name) would consider important and, from those, decide which one or two would be the most important for this character. Support your decisions by explaining what _____ (character's name) says or does in the novel which would indicate the value is important to him or her. *Be as specific as possible and support your opinion with evidence from the novel. Find as much evidence as you can to build a strong case for your choices. You may find it useful to quote directly from the novel.*

Values

Achievement	Physical Appearance
Aesthetics	Pleasure
Altruism	Power or control of other people
Autonomy	Recognition for your accomplishments
Creativity	Religion
Emotional well-being	Skill
Health	Wealth
Justice	Wisdom
Knowledge	_____ (other)
Love	_____ (other)
Loyalty	_____ (other)
Morality	

Note: The actual assignment sheet provides room for students to write responses after each value.

This assignment can be effective as an evaluation of how well students understand the values and beliefs of characters, and can help them to understand the motivation for characters' actions; it can also be used as a preliminary step for other assignments. For example, the character assessment sheet could be used as a prewriting activity for a composition on character motivation and/or character development.

I have also used this assignment as a group activity. Students filled out the sheet individually and then worked in groups to reach consensus about the values of characters in the novel. Since students had already committed themselves in writing prior to getting into the groups, they strongly advocated for the selections they had made, thus necessitating a search of the novel for strong support of their position.

Ronald Barron, Richfield High School, Richfield, Minnesota

Pilgrim Portraits

Students of every age, even high school seniors, find inspiration in a fresh set of markers or crayons. Through the years I have used a number of "coloring projects" for all grade levels, but the most successful has been this activity for seniors.

When we begin our study of Chaucer's "The Prologue to the Canterbury Tales," I read aloud the description of the Knight. As I read, I draw a stick figure of a knight on butcher paper. I use different symbolic representations for each of his traits and add as many details as possible. For example, I draw his right hand with three fingers up in a "scouts honor" sign to signify his honor; I give him a large heart for his "greatness of heart"; and in a cartoon bubble coming from his lips are the words "No lie" to illustrate his dedication to truth. My students laugh at my obvious lack of artistic talent, but by the time we have finished with the Knight's description, they are familiar with his character traits. I emphasize to the students that artistic ability is *not* of consequence here. When my drawing of the Knight's horse looks more like a dog, we simply label it "horse" in large letters.

Occasionally I will draw the Squire also, but usually the students are anxious to begin their own drawings. I divide them into pairs and assign each group the task of drawing one or two of the pilgrims. Armed with butcher paper and markers they begin to create. I invite the students to refer to my teacher's manual and several other references if they need help in deciphering Chaucer's language. We usually spend two class periods working on the drawings. Beginning on the third day, each group orally presents their work, reading the description from the text and showing the representations of the various character traits on their drawing. We display the artwork on the wall for the duration of the unit.

The students enjoy this activity, it alleviates the tedium of simply reading through the material, and it sparks a spirit of competition to see which group can be most complete in their portrait. The drawings also brighten the room and prompt my other classes to say, "When do *we* get to color?"

Mary M. McCoy, Marana High School, Tucson, Arizona

Opening the Literature Circle to the Cassette

I have found that audiocassettes can be a valuable tool to engage students in in-depth literature analysis.

My first use of cassettes in my seventh-grade literature classroom came about by accident. During one of my regular trips to the bookstore, I found a cassette featuring author Ray Bradbury reading his short story "The Veldt" (produced by Mind's Eye). Since my class was going to read the story, I decided to have them listen to the cassette in class. Their challenge was to listen carefully to the opening five minutes of the tape and then write down as precisely as they could the text of the story which inspired the cassette.

I provided two five-minute listening sessions and then gave students time to transcribe their versions of the story which they heard on the tape. After the students had had an opportunity to write their approximations of the written text based on the audiocassette, I distributed copies of "The Veldt," which appears in Bradbury's collection *The Illustrated Man.* When the students had finished, I had asked them to comment on the ways in which the written text compared and contrasted with the spoken cassette version. Since the cassette version of "The Veldt" had a different opening from the printed story, the students had much to comment on. They quickly detailed the many deviations in the cassette from the printed text.

Once the students had enumerated all the differences in the audio and listed the additional sound effects and music Bradbury had included, I asked them why Mr. Bradbury, who produced the audio version of his own cassette, would have opted to make such radical changes in his text.

After students had had a few minutes to think, we talked about the ways in which reading is different from listening, and about what Ray Bradbury might have been trying to accomplish with some of the changes made in the audio version of his story. Many students agreed with Bradbury's decisions, based on the differences between the spoken medium and the printed medium. However, some of the students felt that Bradbury had made the wrong decisions when he transferred his story to audiocassette format. These students developed their own audiocassette scripts for "The Veldt." They were so enthused about these scripts that they voluntarily taped their versions complete with sound effects. We shared both the students' cassettes and the author-produced cassette tape with a colleague's English class. My students were delighted when a few of the other class members liked their tape over Bradbury's production.

The students rerecorded their initial scripts to enhance their production values. They were so pleased with their improvements that they sent a copy of the tape to Ray Bradbury himself. I was delighted to observe how hard they had worked to make their audio version of the story a viable "spoken" transformation of the written text. As I received the meeting notes of their "story transfers" sessions and the drafts of their audio script, I noted their close analysis of the text and images in the printed story of "The Veldt." The spoken cassette scripts they prepared accurately incorporated story themes, plot lines, and dialogue into the audio format. The italicized directions and notes for actor inflections reflected appropriate interpretation of the printed text.

During my conferences with the students about their scripts they initiated their own "improvements" over the commercially produced Bradbury version. They expressed a goal of creating the "correct" and "true" audio version of the story.

In subsequent classes I have drawn on this tool by challenging my students to create a library of audio originals with the goal of being "true" to the printed texts. Our library still lacks an audio version of Emily Dickinson's poetry, however. When I offered to share some commercial cassettes of Dickinson's works as an introduction to our creating an audio version of them, one of my students said: "No, she's too quiet and personal. Let's leave Emily in print."

This kind of sensitivity is the most powerful argument for opening the classroom literature circle to the cassette. Through the cassette medium students can enhance the listening, recording, relating, and interpretation skills which promote literacy and reading.

Rose Reissmann, Community School District #1, Brooklyn, New York

Using Fictional Voice in Literary Analysis

This assignment helps students gain an understanding of characterization and voice, and provides experience in analyzing a text. I ask students to analyze the author's writing using a voice other than their own. They can do this by having a fictional character analyze another character; by having a fictional character analyze the author's craft as a writer (characterization, plot structure, syntax, diction, symbolism, point of view, motifs); or by having a fictional character recommend alternatives or illustrate similarities/differences to his or her own characterization.

I have used this approach with an assortment of texts and require that students use this format in at least one critical analysis paper per term. When students have finished their reading I ask them to generate their own topics for this assignment. In class discussion we reflect on all of the texts read to date and look for interesting pairings. The following is a list of some of their ideas for three texts.

Yellow Raft in Blue Water by Michael Dorris

1. Hamlet speaks to Christine about fate (destiny), suicide, death, attitudes toward the past, relationships with parents, the legacies left by a parent.
2. Amanda Wingfield (*The Glass Menagerie*) speaks to Dorris about his treatment of Christine and Ida.
3. Holden Caulfield (*The Catcher in the Rye*) speaks to Ray about rights of passage.
4. Tom Wingfield (*The Glass Menagerie*) discusses Ida's servitude to family or Christine's lack of servitude. He could also discuss the topic of escape in regards to the two women.

5. Ray, Christine, or Ida speaks to Dorris about his treatment of her character.

6. Polonius (*Hamlet*) speaks to Christine or Rayona about how children should behave and offers Rayona advice specific to her needs.

7. Ophelia (*Hamlet*) speaks to Christine about how men are portrayed in the novel.

8. Elgin or Dayton speak to Dorris about his treatment of men in the novel.

9. Maxine Hong Kingston (*Woman Warrior*) speaks to all three women about how they deny each other the stories of their pasts.

10. Sara Smolinsky (*Bread Givers*) speaks to Christine about leaving and returning.

11. Nyasha and Tambo (*Nervous Conditions*) speak to Rayona about cultural heritage.

12. Esperanza (*House on Mango Street*) compares Dorris's depiction of the reservation with her definition of home.

A Doll's House by Henrik Ibsen

1. Janie (*Their Eyes Were Watching God*) discusses Nora's relationship with Helmer.

2. Edward Rochester (*Jane Eyre*) condemns Nora for abandoning her husband and children.

3. Brave Orchid (*Woman Warrior*) analyzes Nora's behavior toward her domineering husband.

4. Dr. Rank compares his relationship with Nora to that of Nora and Helmer.

5. Sara Smolinsky (*Bread Givers*) instructs Nora on exploring one's potential.

6. Antoinette Cosway (*Wide Sargasso Sea*) explores Ibsen's views on marriage.

7. Nel Wright or Sula Peace (*Sula*) instruct Nora on the past's impact on the present.

Catcher in the Rye by J. D. Salinger

1. Esperanza (*House on Mango Street*) analyzes Holden as a symbol of all children in search of answers to life's mysteries.

2. Simon (*Lord of the Flies*) discusses Holden's isolation and loneliness.

3. Naomi Nakane (*Obasan*) instructs Holden on the need for community, connectedness.

4. Lyman Lamartine (*Love Medicine*) compares Salinger's characterization of Holden to his own characterization.

5. Antigone or Hamlet challenge Holden's motives for "dropping out."

6. Sara Smolinsky (*Bread Givers*) compares Holden's attitude toward women with that of the men in her story.

Charon Tierney, Willmar High School, Willmar, Minnesota

3 Explorations

Our favorite classroom activities are often students' favorites as well, probably because they tend to be lively, stimulating assignments that engage the minds of both students and teachers and create a special sense of classroom community. This section includes some favorite teaching ideas, all of which are explorations of one sort or another—explorations of metaphorical language, of students' cultural backgrounds, of multiple perspectives on the news, and more.

Culture, Quilts, and Community

For the past few years I have required my high school students to research their cultural backgrounds, family traditions, and heritage. This task involves communication with parents, grandparents, and other relatives. Students are to listen to stories from the past, take notes on genealogical background, if available, and recall or question relatives regarding family stories from the past. Then, they produce a composition that reflects what they have learned. Last, students participate in a show-and-tell relating their findings. These have included passing around photographs of outlaw and Indian chief relatives, listening to recordings of grandparents as they tell of a particularly hard winter, and eating Bohemian kolaches and Hungarian cabbage rolls.

This past school year I added a new component to the project. I solicited the assistance of the local quilting guild to prepare unbleached muslin blocks for the students to design an individual quilt block to represent the results of their research on culture, tradition, and/or heritage. My students were not skilled in the art of sewing, but they all could draw and paint symbols and/or pictures onto the muslin blocks. This educational partnership with the Muskogee Quilters Guild allowed the guild the opportunity to fulfill their mission of sharing the importance of quilting as a treasured art form. The students gained valuable knowledge on the importance of preserving the past through discussion, through writing, and through quilt making.

The students each donated $4.25 for the paint, brushes, muslin, and fabric to piece the blocks together. (A class bake sale or car wash could provide funds as well.) I picked up fabric samples from a local quilting shop for the classes to select the fabric. The owner of the shop, a quilting guild member, charged my students her cost for the fabric and donated her time to cut and piece the blocks, and bind and tie the quilt when we were finished. She advised the class on fabric content, on the size of the blocks, and on the number needed to complete the quilt. For example, my second-hour class had twenty-one students. With those blocks, a class dedication block, a teacher block, and the guild block, their quilt consisted of twenty-four blocks, four across and six down. Each block was cut to 15" × 15", reserving a one-inch margin around one edge.

Preparation was the most crucial component of the painting project. I was apprehensive about the potential mess involved in painting in the classroom. I had purchased the fabric paints and brushes from a local hobby store and brought paper cups and buckets for water to clean the brushes and paper towels for cleanup. I also informed the custodian of what I was doing. (I've found that it's always helpful to get the assistance of support personnel in projects that affect them in their jobs.)

The two days we spent in class on the actual painting were focused and productive. The students, some with the help of their parents, designed the blocks on paper and transferred them onto the muslin to be painted. I encouraged parental input because the research depended upon the support of the family. I also invited the local newspaper, which sent a reporter and a photographer to my class to report on the project. An article followed on the front page the next day.

On the two painting days the students were very serious and possessive of their blocks. They discussed with each other what colors and symbols might better present their messages. They shared brushes of different sizes. Some even helped each other at the end of the second day to meet the classroom deadline. Three students from the two participating classes had to take their blocks and paints home to finish. My apprehension over the potential mess was unwarranted. I set aside the last five minutes of each class period for cleanup. Wet painted blocks lay on the tables, bookshelves, and counters to dry. One student from each class volunteered to paint the class dedication block for the quilt at home for extra credit.

After all the blocks for each class were designed, painted, and dried, I delivered them to the quilting guild, whose members pieced them together with the fabric the students had chosen. Once the quilts were bound and tied into beautiful culture quilts, the students then received invitations from local civic organizations to present programs to share their stories and their quilts. My first-hour class received an invitation from the father of one student to present a program for the noon Rotary Club. Our community's business leaders were delighted to see the quilt and to hear the stories the students pulled from their compositions about their research. I introduced the project to the Rotarians, and the students followed displaying their blocks and reading passages from their compositions about their family heritage or traditions. Lynne shared her block with the Buick symbol, a school house and bell, and the German name Wagner. She told the story of her family's German heritage, pronouncing her last name Wagner with a "V" instead of the "W." Heather shared her French family tradition of decorating shoes with fruit underneath the Christmas tree. Jenny told of her ancestor's home in Beverly, Massachusetts, built in 1637 and still owned by the family. Gabe explained the dedication block he designed for the class. Surrounded by flags of the world, a replica of the United States—with Muskogee starred—blends with the global map of the world signifying how all cultures have melted into the United States and, in particular, into the community of Muskogee, Oklahoma.

Some students could not connect their ancestral past to present traditions as easily as others. For instance, Michele designed her block using the continent of Africa as an outline blending the colors of African flags within the continent. She is proud of her African ancestry, but had difficulty finding details of her family history to make that connection. In her composition, she described her mother's wild onions and scrambled eggs, fried chicken, and biscuits—a traditional Memorial Day meal served after her family spruces up the cemetery in Wybark, Oklahoma, the town where her mother was born.

The students debated over what they would do with their quilt. They discussed several options, including a raffle, but decided to donate the quilts to the school library as permanent wall hangings accompanied by the photographs and the folder of compositions. A guild volunteer prepared the quilts for hanging, and the principal and librarian arranged for the display.

The project was a successful venture into personal research, community, business partnership, writing, art, and oral presentation. It was more than an academic unit. The students began to see one another as individuals with special talents and as friends who appreciate their differences and their similarities.

Sandra J. Brewer, Muskogee High School, Muskogee, Oklahoma

Life Is a Metaphor

Some students find the notion of metaphorical language intimidating or discomforting—largely, I suspect, because they rarely identify (or have pointed out to them) metaphors outside the context of published professional writing.

As a way of demystifying the metaphor, I offer three common items for the consideration of the class, such as a stapler, a box of paper clips, and a pack of index cards. (I like to vary the items used so that they do not grow stale for me—and so I can identify more challenging and more fruitful items for future use.)

Next, I write "Life is a _____." on the board, and I ask the class to select one of the three items to complete the sentence. Usually, a couple of students will call out a choice and we will check for consensus, but occasionally they are more reserved, so we delay a final selection until we've gone a little further. (Sometimes we keep working with all three.)

The next step is to explain how the selected item can be a metaphor for life. We brainstorm these but do not record the responses on the board. Common responses for the stapler, for example, include notions like "You have to push it to get it to do what you want," "It makes things stick together," and "You have to put things into it if you expect to get anything out of it." Once a few suggestions are made, this generally flows well.

Before we lose momentum, I shift their attention back to the phrase on the board and, telling them to disgregard the three objects previously considered, ask them to brainstorm a list of items to complete the metaphor. I anticipate some hackneyed responses, like "highway," but by insisting that we fill the board, I ensure that selections cover quite a range in terms of their depth. If we seem to run dry, sometimes offering the simile version, "Life is like a _____." gives a slight— but productive—shift of perspective. (Forrest Gump's mother was especially helpful in this respect.)

After the board has been filled, I ask the students to form small groups of three or four. The groups are then to select the metaphor (or simile) they like best and brainstorm (and record) as many statements as they can which demonstrate, clarify, or illustrate the metaphor. These are then shared with the rest of the class.

The most satisfying benefit of this exercise is seeing the complexity of thoughts that flow almost painlessly. A side benefit of no small consequence is that the exercise has stimulated some students to go on to produce pieces of creative writing—especially poetry.

W. David LeNoir, Western Kentucky University, Bowling Green, Kentucky

Photo ID

This is a great back-to-school activity to help the students get to know one another, plus it uses the skill of interviewing. It is adapted from the interview technique by Linda Rief in *Seeking Diversity,* and I have added my own suggestions.

Each student must have a partner. You can assign partners or do it at random. It works best if the two partners don't know one another well. Explain that the purpose of the photo ID is to interview each other and to work jointly using that information to create a "photo-biographical" sketch. Give each student two 5" × 8" index cards or use notebook paper instead. Fold the cards or paper in half and number each half 1, 2, 3, and 4. Tell them to write down on side 1 at least five questions to ask their partner to help them get to know them better. If you want their photo IDs to follow the same pattern, you can give them the same five prompts, such as favorite author or book, favorite movie, favorite food, what I want to be when I grow up, what I like best about myself. Next, they should begin the interview process by asking their partner their questions and recording the answers on side 2. Then they should pick one thing that they learned about each other that they wish to know more about. On side 3 they list five more questions that focus on that particular item. Then they ask their partner those questions and record their answers on

side 4. While the students are interviewing one another, I find a "picture-perfect" spot in the room and call them up individually to take their photograph.

Give each student a piece of 9" × 12" colored construction paper. Working with their partner, they should list on the construction paper the pertinent and interesting information from their research. My students followed the same format so that the photo IDs were easier to understand. It is important to list the facts in each of the four corners of the paper, leaving room for the photograph. I also had them list four adjectives that would describe their partner and write these around the photo. Then they illustrated the IDs using markers or crayons.

It will take several days to do this properly. We interviewed one day, designed and illustrated the next, and mounted the photo on a third. To prevent damage to or loss of IDs, students did not work on this at home, and I kept the IDs until completion. Then we "published" by posting them on the bulletin board and around the room.

This is a great icebreaker and impresses parents on Back-to-School Night!

Patti Trudell, Broadmoor Middle Lab School, Shreveport, Louisiana

Meeting of Minds Project

Steve Allen is well known as a television star, musician, comedian, author, and political activist, but for me his greatest professional accomplishment is as an educator. It took eighteen years for network television to realize that America could appreciate his visionary concept for a series, and in 1977 PBS aired the first of Allen's *Meeting of Minds* program. To me this twenty-four episode series remains as one of television's finest.

While the roundtable discussion has long been common television fare, Allen put his own twist on that format. On *Meeting of Minds,* he served as host/moderator to famous people from disparate professions, places, and eras. One by one, these luminaries, portrayed by appropriately costumed actors, were introduced and engaged in skillfully scripted, "impromptu" discussions. On one show, for example, Galileo Galilei, Emily Dickinson, Atilla the Hun, and Charles Darwin expressed their views on such subjects as natural selection, reclusive behavior, and the teachings of Aristotle.

This was the inspiration for a project I did with my ninth graders. We did it during the second half of the school year so that the class would have a background of various poems, short stories, and novels from our curriculum. Before the students began their active involvement, I provided each of them with a *Meeting of Minds* script, which they were to read first. Next, in an effort to ensure a mix of personalities, I divided the class into groups of five, each of which then selected characters, one per group member, from our literary readings. (Before they made their selections, however, I suggested that they consider what possible commonalities their characters might have with the others, remaining true to the literary originals.)

Each group's job was to write and perform (preferably in costume) a five- to seven-minute script of a conversation among their chosen characters. Additionally, in the finished scripts, the students had to have every character reflect in the conversation on a theme, plot, or message from the work from which she or he came. Because each group scripted its own conversation, it did not matter if two or three other groups had selected one or more of the same characters. In fact, it was quite fascinating to see how different groups handled the same character.

This is a project that needs substantial class time for writing and revising the scripts as well as for rehearsing. Although I did not require the students to memorize the dialogue for their presentations, the performances generally went quite smoothly because most of the students relied only sparingly on notes written on three-by-five cards. These ninth graders were aware of the requirements from the beginning of the project, so they knew one grade would be given to the whole group for the script and another to individuals for their performances. In spite of the fact that all of this was rather time consuming, the students took with them a remarkable, memorable learning experience.

Jeff Roth, Abington Junior High School, Abington, Pennsylvania

Great Lovers

The model competency-based language arts program in our state encourages the integration of reading, writing, listening/visual literacy, and oral communication as we develop units to implement the district's curriculum. This project, which has been used successfully as part of a unit with love as the unifying theme, provides that integration. It also encourages research that leads to a form of writing other than a report or a term paper.

With this assignment I provide the following guidelines: With your partner, research a famous couple. Write a skit based on your research to present to the class. You and your partner will portray the couple. Take careful note of when the couple lived and how they looked so that you can be appropriately costumed for your presentation. Prepare a bibliography of the sources you used for your information.

Some suggestions:

Duke and Duchess of Windsor

John Smith and Pocahontas

Caesar and Cleopatra

Antony and Cleopatra

Napoleon and Josephine

Dr. Martin Luther King and Coretta Scott King

Andrew and Rachel Jackson

F. Scott and Zelda Fitzgerald

Juan and Eva Peron

Percy and Mary Shelley
Edgar Allan Poe and Virginia
Elizabeth Barrett and Robert Browning
Bonnie Parker and Clyde Barrow
John Lennon and Yoko Ono
Ruby Dee and Ossie Davis
Olivia Langdon and Samuel Clemens
Joe DiMaggio and Marilyn Monroe
George and Martha Washington
Mumtaz Mahal and Shah Jahan
Humphrey Bogart and Lauren Bacall

When students have written and rehearsed their skits, they present them to an appreciative audience. Skit content and tone have ranged from the serious and romantic to the slapstick and sarcastic. Ideally, the skits would be videotaped for posterity, but even without this step, this project provides strong motivation for research, writing, and oral presentation.

Mary Knisely Reith, Theodore Roosevelt High School, Kent, Ohio

Tools of the Trade: Sidewalk Chalk and Rubber Stamps

I have long admired elementary school teachers for the imaginative ways they find to make learning fun for their students. I recently began using two "toys" with my high school students with much success.

I like to give my students frequent opportunities to read in class, both silently and to others. When students read silently, it becomes apparent that reading speed varies tremendously. I wanted to provide a creative way to reinforce the reading for those quick readers without disturbing students who needed more time to complete the story. My solution—sidewalk chalk! One of my students gave me a bag of this chunky, colored chalk, and now we use it to illustrate parts of the stories. When a student finishes reading, he or she may move to one of the many blackboards in my classroom and, using the sidewalk chalk, illustrate any section of the story which seems to create a vivid image. Sometimes I even ask students to illustrate a particular scene because I am not sure each reader visualizes it in the same fashion. I used this technique, for example, with Dickens's short story, "The Signalman," to see how well the students visualized the railroad, tunnel, and signal hut details. It has been great fun to watch students who are silently engrossed in a story awake to the pleasure of a room of illustrations.

I know that rubber stamps have been popular tools of the trade among elementary teachers for years, but now I use them as reminders with my older students. Often, students ask me to look over a draft of a paper that is giving them difficulty. I like to read many of these during my planning period so that students can continue to work on them for homework. Now when a student hands me a draft, hoping that I will read it during the day, I stamp their hand with one of my many rubber stamps and students rarely forget to pick up their paper before they leave school. The stamps have proven so successful that any time a forgetful student needs a gentle reminder of any kind, we get the stamps out.

High school students pride themselves on their sophistication, but I have found that when it comes to using chalk to draw on the blackboard or going home with a Donald Duck stamp on their hands, they are all still kids at heart!

Judy Champney, Science Hill High School, Johnson City, Tennessee

Multiple Perspectives Newsreading

In an effort to enhance my students' daily newsreading, I decided to add another conversant to what was usually a two-party, student-to-student discussion on the news. Why not get someone from the students' home, a family member, neighbor, or community member—preferably someone from another generation—to add their perspective? As I considered the rich diverse cultural backgrounds of my students, including some from newly arrived immigrant and nonnative English language speaking homes, I realized that the students could easily tap into varied perspectives that would enhance their comprehension and reflection about the news.

I introduced this project to my students by telling them that their homework was going to involve getting a homework partner to share the task. Since many of the students' family members were often not available in the afternoon or evening (because of jobs, school, or because they were not living in the same place the students were), the students were also allowed to partner with an older sibling (three or more years older) or relative, a neighbor, or even a school employee (a teacher, aide, secretary, custodian). It was suggested that the perspective of someone not born in the United States or someone who did not speak English was not only acceptable but desirable. This would provide the U.S. student with a "global" perspective on the news.

The students helped design the format for the newsreading worksheet (see page 53). Once the format was decided, the worksheet was word processed and photocopied each week. The students' weekly task was to select an article of their own choice, react to it, and then share it with their designated partner. If they wished, the students could choose a major ongoing news story, a neighborhood news story, or a story from a foreign language newspaper.

I was surprised by the range of stories and news issues selected initially by the students and then in subsequent weeks by their partners. Among them: a young mother who lost custody of her child because she put the child in day care while she attended college classes; a neighborhood murder which was only covered extensively in the local newspapers; a story about nuns, who taught in parochial schools, and their health care concerns; a feature on aerobic exercises; a feature about a sixteen-year-old Ukrainian immigrant and her experiences adjusting to life in the United States; and an interview with the leader of the Urban League in which racism as a poverty factor was discussed.

Depending on the time available, the students were usually given a chance to do a classroom "read through" of their news story and reactions. Unlike other read-aloud opportunities, this one allowed students to spontaneously add in explanations and reactions to the pieces they were sharing.

For instance, one student said that her mother, who had kept her in a neighborhood day care center when she was preschool-age, was very upset by the article about the young mother losing custody of her child. The student said her mom had picked the article out for their share talks, even though it was not a story that would have interested the student at all.

Worksheet

Multiple Perspectives Newsreading

Student Name: _____

Partner Name: _____

Other personal details you'd like to share (you need not fill this out if you don't want to): age, ethnic background, cultural background, job background, relationship to your "partner" _____

_____

News Item Selected (paper, title, reporter/columnist): _____

_____

Date of News Item: _____

Paste or Clip News Item Here

_____

Who selected the piece? _____ Student _____ Multiple Perspectives Partner

Why was this piece chosen? _____

Partner's Reactions _____

_____

_____

Student's Reactions _____

_____

_____

Other information/"Interesting Stuff." (Will you follow this story? Were either of you surprised, happy, pleased, or upset by the other's reaction? Has either of your perspectives on this piece changed?)

The mother wrote, "The article is sending a mixed message to mothers throughout the United States. On one hand, we tell women to get off public assistance and get training to gain useful skills. But now we are telling women that if they send their children to day care while they further their education, the fathers will receive custody. I strongly disagree with this article because my two best friends became pregnant at eighteen years old. Like me they needed to send their children to day care so they could provide for them. If a man provides for his children, he's considered a good parent and gets respect; a woman loses her child."

The students' perspective as a twelve-year-old on this was: "First off I would never pick this story. But my mom made me realize how important this case is for women who must take care of their children and make money for them. Why would a judge give the father custody if the woman leaves her baby with a babysitter or at day care? The woman wanted to get an education so she could make a good life for herself and her child. If she stayed home, how would she make money. Off welfare?"

Several students' commentaries were reactions and responses to the concerns of the people they talked to, rather than immediate personal reactions to particular news events. Myra read an interview with a sixteen-year-old Ukrainian immigrant named Raimonda discussing how her life in the United States was different from her life in the Ukraine. Myra said she picked the article because "the headline 'This Is My Country Now' sounds just like what my Grandma is always saying when she finishes telling me how she had to work in China. Sometimes she just stops talking about China and how you had to be your family's daughter and husband's wife there. She says, 'here, you have a chance and the freedom to do and be, whatever you want to be.' That sounded just like what Raimonda said. I wanted to read this story to my Grandma, who can't read English newspapers."

Myra's grandmother's comments (as translated by Myra): "Even though this girl she come from the Ukraine, she knows what I know, how to survive in America. Here you have a chance to be who you want to be, not who your father was or your husband is. I, too, would like to go back to China, but I fear it. This is my country now."

As the students shared both their response to the news articles and their selected "partner's" reaction, they discussed each event and included comments demonstrating a critique or siding with one or both of the perspectives. Occasionally one of the adults who was really interested in a particular news story came to talk with the class, including one student's mother, who was suing for a bartender job traditionally reserved for a man, and another student's cousin, who had undergone DNA tests to find a suitable bone marrow transplant donor.

Within two months, we were able to publish a News Views Magazine offering culturally diverse, cross-generational reactions to sexual harassment, college tuition, asbestos, subway crime, health care, random violence, unemployment, Whitewater, political parties, the Power Rangers, *Forrest Gump, The Lion King,* and Princess Di. Not only did the students themselves often stick with one story or issue for several weeks, but they and their partners often purposely expanded the required dual responses to include a broader range of individuals.

The ongoing partnerships were often valued by older partners as well. Several retirees who participated as partners wrote to tell me and their student co-commentators how much they enjoyed talking about the news and hearing how "young people felt." One grandmother said she had "lost" her grandson as he got older and stayed out with his friends, but that the project had given them a chance to sit down and talk again.

While the pilot project does not purport to be a comprehensive program, it has value as one small step toward what can and must be an ongoing parent, community, and school exercise in proactive conversation across generations. As students go beyond the classroom to examine, contemplate, and critique current concerns with other community members, school-based skills and curricula core are put to use in the real world. The students, adults, and teachers who participate in this exercise will all be the richer for it.

Rose Reissmann, Community School District #1, Brooklyn, New York

Define Your Terms

Students sometimes don't understand what information is called for in study questions or on tests. Many different terms are used when asking students to think and write about what they've learned, and some of them may be unfamiliar to students or may bear confusing similarities to one another. This assignment helps senior high school students understand the nuances among such terms and concepts.

Start by giving students this list of terms:

analyze	illustrate
be specific	interpret
compare	justify
condense	list
contrast	mention
criticize	name
define	outline
describe	quote
discuss	refer to
enumerate	sketch
evaluate	stress
explain	summarize
give examples	

Pairs or small groups of students take two to four terms each. (There will probably need to be overlap, with different groups covering some of the same terms.) Group members first jot down what they think the terms mean and then look up the actual meanings in a dictionary or consult the list of definitions provided below. After comparing and contrasting the terms among themselves, they present their words to the class, highlighting the similarities and differences among them and, where possible, supplying examples of how each term might be used.

The following definitions are taken from *Webster's Ninth New Collegiate Dictionary.*

analyze   to study or determine the nature and relationship of the parts of by analysis

be specific   specific: constituting or falling into a specifiable category

compare   to examine the character or qualities of, especially in order to discover resemblances or differences

condense   to make denser or more compact

contrast   to set off in contrast: compare or appraise in respect to differences

criticize   to consider the merits and demerits of and judge accordingly; evaluate

define   to discover and set forth the meaning of (as a word); to make distinct, clear, or detailed in outline

describe   to represent or give an account of in words

discuss   to present in detail for examination or consideration; to talk about

enumerate   to ascertain the number of; to specify one after another; list

evaluate   to determine or fix the value of; to determine the significance or worth of, usually by careful appraisal and study

explain   to make plain or understandable; to give the reason for or cause of; to show the logical development or relationships of

give examples   to present one that serves as a pattern to be imitated or not to be imitated; to present a single item, fact, incident, or aspect that is representative of all of a group or type; to present an instance (as a problem to be solved) serving to illustrate a rule or precept or to act as an exercise in the application of a rule

illustrate   to make clear by giving or serving as an example or instance; to show clearly; demonstrate; to give an example or instance

interpret   to explain or tell the meaning of; present in understandable terms

justify   to prove or show to be just, right, or reasonable

list   enumerate; to include on a list; register

mention   the act or instance of citing or calling attention to someone or something, especially in a casual or incidental manner

name   to mention or identify by name (a word or phrase that constitutes the distinctive designation of a person or thing)

outline   a condensed treatment of a particular subject; a summary of a written work; a preliminary account of a project

quote   to speak or write (a passage) from another, usually with credit acknowledgment; to repeat a passage from, especially in substantiation or illustration; to give exact information on

refer to   to think of, regard, or classify within a general cause; to allot to a particular place, stage, or period; to regard as coming from or located in a specific area; to direct attention, usually by clear and specific mention

sketch   a tentative draft (as for a literary work); a brief description (as of a person) or outline; a short literary composition somewhat resembling the short story and the essay but intentionally slight in treatment, discursive in style, and familiar in tone

stress place emphasis or weight on

summarize to tell in, or reduce to, a summary; to make a summary; summary: covering the main points succinctly

This assignment not only helps students understand distinctions among important terms and concepts but can also increase students' confidence when they are faced with study questions or exams.

Sylvia Slack, McGavock High School, Nashville, Tennessee

Indexes

Author Index

Subject Index

Classroom Management

Discussion

Interdisciplinary

Language Exploration

Literature